Panda and the Magic Soap

Written by Ida Sabitsana-Corpus

Illustrated by Marie Javier Pert

Edited by Jill Sabitsana

To my parents, Tatay Edsa and Mama Carmel, for inspiring me to live a simple and authentic life.
- Krissy

To my family, especially my mum and dad - Ell and Leslie. Thank you for being the best cheerleaders since day one.
- Marie

First paperback edition June 2022
First hardcover edition June 2022

Illustrations © Marie Javier Pert

ISBN 978-0-473-63500-8 (paperback)
ISBN 978-0-473-63501-5 (hardcover)

Published by Maria Ida Teresa S. Corpus
Country of production: New Zealand

Hello, it's me!
I'm Panda your friend!
Today, let's play
A game of pretend.

Chameleon, my pal,
Did something amazing.
His colors would change,
As if they were fading.

I'm plain, bland, and boring.
Is that all I'll be?
Only black and white
Li-ter-a-lly!

Chameleon said, "Use this magic soap,
While thinking of a hue,
Wait until it bubbles,
Soon there'll be a new you."

So I went out for a walk
To meet my colorful neighbors.
Let's start the game
Of changing colors!

scrub...

scrub...

scrub...

Green, clever CROCODILE
As still as a log.

Brown, playful HOUND
Does the downward dog.

Blue, careful STARFISH
Stretches her arms in the air.

Orange, bold LION
Sighs without a care.

Hey look, red BUTTERFLY
I have spots just like you!

Pink, balancing FLAMINGO
Who only wears one shoe?

Yellow, busy GIRAFFE
Stretches his neck up high.

Phew! That was tiring!
Now I think I'll say goodbye.

Oh, I must say,
It's been a busy day.
My neighbors looked amused.
But not me, I was confused.

I've changed to all colors.
Some were dark,
Some were light.
Every color was special.
Every hue a delight.

Chameleon, today was magical.
Thank you, but nope.
I have realized something,
I don't need your magic soap.

I followed my heart.
Listened to my inner voice.
This is who I am.
This is my choice.

My black and white
I will proudly display.
I love my birthday suit!
It is here to stay.

the end

The author

Ida Sabitsana-Corpus was born and raised in Manila, Philippines, where she earned her bachelor's degree in Early Childhood Education from De La Salle University.

Ida is a preschool teacher who encourages play and movement through interactive storytelling. She likes to keep an active lifestyle and explore the outdoors with her family. She also enjoys listening to music, munching on snacks, and taking long naps.

She lives in Napier, New Zealand with her husband and their two kids.

The illustrator

Marie is a mum of 2, a kindergarten teacher, and a freelance illustrator. Following her passion for children's literature and teaching, she later took up a degree in Reading education at Ateneo de Manila University in the Philippines.

She recently started Coos & Boos, an online digital art shop. Her favourite things to do are drawing, spending time with loved ones, and drinking a nice cup of coffee.

She currently resides in Wellington, New Zealand with her family.